GRA

TO LIFE

EMILY BIGGERS

BARBOUR
PUBLISHING

ISBN 978-1-60260-829-0

Published by Barbour Publishing, Inc., P.O. Box 719, Uhrichsville, Ohio 44683, www.barbourbooks.com

Our mission is to publish and distribute inspirational products offering exceptional value and biblical encouragement to the masses.

ecpa Member of the
Evangelical Christian
Publishers Association

Printed in the United States of America.

INTRODUCTION

Congratulations! You did it. You graduated! You set a goal, accomplished it, walked across the stage, and received your diploma. . . . Now what?

This book is designed to guide you as you step into the next chapter of your life. Each section focuses on a relevant aspect of life that recent graduates face. Along with a short devotion, you will find related scriptures as well as tips and tricks that may be helpful. Also, sprinkled throughout the book are words of advice from other recent graduates. Their words are from the heart. They were written with you in mind.

Remember as you move forward that God is with you. He promises to lead, guide, and protect His children. You may wish to read one section of *Grad's Guide to Life* each day. You may prefer to take it slower, allowing yourself time to ponder upon the guidance provided. Select a couple of scriptures per section to memorize. Go before the Lord and submit the area of your life that the book is addressing that day.

The words of this book are a gift to you, graduate. May they inspire you to face your future with confidence and grace!

The LORD will guide you continually.
ISAIAH 58:11 NKJV

CONTENTS

I Believe:
Owning My Faith

My relationship with Jesus Christ is my end-all, be-all. Without Christ in my life I would be nothing; He is my strength, my rock, my fortress, and deliverer. However, it wasn't until my freshman year of college when I moved away from home and everyone that I knew that I really came to fully and completely depend on God with every breath that I took. Even though I was born and raised in a Christian home and family setting, realizing that I am not in control of my life is what allowed me to own my faith but also enabled me to have an active, dependent relationship with God.

EMILY HOERNSCHEMEYER, 20

Whether you are heading to college or starting a new job, your life will be different after graduation. Tossing that cap into the air symbolized not only an ending, but also a new beginning. As Dr. Seuss would say, "Oh the places you'll go!"

Graduation marks a milestone in your life and opens up possibilities for you. It's exciting, but at the same time it may be overwhelming to face so many choices and changes at once. Now is the time to be sure you know what you believe and truly own your faith.

Consider the difference between religion and relationship. Religion is made up of traditions and doctrines, while a relationship is personal, living, and growing. Which does God desire? Of course, as a loving heavenly Father, He longs to have a relationship with His children. He tells us to "be still and know that I am God." We tend to forget the "be still" part, don't we? Life gets busy, but setting aside a quiet time to pray and read your Bible will strengthen your walk with God. It will help keep your thoughts and ways aligned with His.

Finding a church where you can worship and grow in the Lord is important. Most churches have groups that meet during the week for Bible study. Church is a great place to develop friendships with other believers.

Think about your passions and abilities. Are you musical or skilled in construction? Do you enjoy children? Serving at church or a mission organization is a great way to use your gifts to honor God, it's a lot of fun, and the blessings are great. Consider teaching children or helping with repairs on homes of the elderly. You can lead others in worship by joining a praise band or choir. A mission trip may provide opportunities for you to assist in planting new churches or working in an orphanage. Matthew 5:16 says "Let your light shine before men in such a way that they may see your good works, and glorify your Father who is in heaven." Service puts action to your faith and points others to God.

Uncertainties are a reality in life, but God has promised never to leave you. Jeremiah 29:11 says that God's plans are to "prosper you and never to bring you harm." Own your faith, act on it, and give God control. Allow Him to sit in the driver's seat. Give Him the wheel. There will be some twists and turns in the road, but you can trust Him to get you where you are going.

God, I ask that You help me as I seek to put You first in my life. I want my choices to reflect that I am Your child. Amen.

When you feel down or depressed, do something for others. Visit an elderly relative, bake cookies for neighbors, or offer to babysit for friends so they can have an evening out on the town. This will shift your focus from your own problems to helping others.

■

"Be still, and know that I am God; I will be exalted among the nations, I will be exalted in the earth."

PSALM 46:10 NIV

■

Start keeping a prayer journal. Record your prayer requests as well as God's answers.

■

For in the gospel a righteousness from God is revealed, a righteousness that is by faith from first to last, just as it is written:"The righteous will live by faith."

ROMANS 1:17 NIV

*But the fruit of the Spirit is love, joy, peace,
patience, kindness, goodness, faithfulness,
gentleness and self-control. Against
such things there is no law.*

GALATIANS 5:22–23 NIV

■

*Keep some note cards with stamps and return address
labels in your desk drawer. Write a note each week to a
friend or relative. Include a scripture verse and a word of
encouragement. Pray specifically for the needs of that
person throughout the week.*

■

*I will praise God's name in song
and glorify him with thanksgiving.*

PSALM 69:30 NIV

■

*Faith is a personal thing, intimate in nature.
You cannot lean on another's faith or
another's walk with Jesus. You must
find your own faith in Christ.*

Purchase a daily devotional book to read during your
quiet time with God. There are devotional books
specifically designed for students,
women, men, singles, etc.

■

We ought always to give thanks to God
for you, brethren, as is only fitting, because your
faith is greatly enlarged, and the love
of each one of you toward one another
grows ever greater.

2 Thessalonians 1:3 nasb

To help you memorize scripture verses, write them on 3x5-inch index cards. Tape a card to your bathroom mirror, car dashboard, or another prominent place. Practice it while getting ready in the morning or driving, etc., until you can say it from memory.

■

You shall love the LORD your God with all your heart and with all your soul and with all your might.

DEUTERONOMY 6:5 NASB

Sign up for a Bible study class. Buy a brightly colored folder to keep your notes in, and put the dates and times of the class on your calendar. These tips will help you remember to do the homework and show up for the study each week.

■

I pray that you, being rooted and established in love, may have power, together with all the saints, to grasp how wide and long and high and deep is the love of Christ, and to know this love that surpasses knowledge—that you may be filled to the measure of all the fullness of God.

EPHESIANS 3:16–19 NIV

■

As the body without the spirit is dead, so faith without deeds is dead.

JAMES 2:26 NIV

*Remember that God's Word speaks of moving
mountains with faith just the size of a tiny
mustard seed. Ask God to take you where
you are and to increase your faith.*

■

*We ask God to give you complete knowledge of his will
and to give you spiritual wisdom and understanding.
Then the way you live will always honor and please the
Lord, and your lives will produce every kind of good fruit.
All the while, you will grow as you learn to
know God better and better.*

COLOSSIANS 1:9–10 NLT

■

*I was on my own for the first time in my life and college
was a great season to search and discover what I believed
for once. Finding a church that became a second family
of mine was crucial in my relationship with the Lord
during college. It's not easy because no one is telling you
to go to church or small group. But my soul longed to be
a part of the body of Christ and it opened many doors
for questions from my nonbeliever friends.*

MOLLY WEISGARBER, 22

New Digs: Adjusting to Different Surroundings

The key to adjusting to a new living situation is trusting and depending on God. When I moved into college my freshman year, He was my comfort, my best friend, and the one constant in my life.

EMILY HOERNSCHEMEYER, 20

You were probably comfortable in your surroundings before graduation. Do you find yourself in a new place now? Everything familiar has been replaced with the unknown. Whether you are living in a dorm, apartment, or a house, with or without roommates, new surroundings can be unsettling. You were used to the creaks in the floor and the drip of the bathroom sink, but there are different noises to adjust to in this new place. Before long, you won't even notice them, but it may take awhile for this to feel like home.

View your new environment as an opportunity! Get out and see what is in the community. Have you located a post office yet? A grocery store? What about a local hole-in-the-wall restaurant? Ask around about fun things to do in the area. Introduce yourself to your neighbors. Go online and search for churches. Choose to find a church right away to get off to a great start. Whatever you do the first weekend you are there will dictate your future patterns.

You will probably be tempted to return to your "old turf" often during the first months. Of course, you don't want to lose touch with family and friends. Keep in mind, though, that you will only get out of your new community as much as you are willing to put into it. What does that mean? It means you need to make a conscious effort to build a life where you are. You may be in a big city or a small town. Both have their advantages. Take in the culture of this new place. Visit area museums and pick a favorite barbeque joint.

Seek out places to meet new people while doing things that you enjoy. Join a gym or sports league. Volunteer at a local homeless shelter, nursing home, or library. If you are a student, many campuses have Christian student unions and student government groups that may interest you. You can also make friends quickly through your church by becoming a part of a weeknight community group or Bible study.

Remember that Jesus experienced the ultimate in adjusting to a new environment. He left heaven's glory for a fallen world and died to save us from sin. He left a throne for a manger bed and gave up angels' praise for carpentry. He knows about change! Have you asked Him to help you to feel comfortable in your new digs?

Thank You, Lord, for this experience and for my new surroundings. Help me to feel at home, adjust easily, and make some new friends. Please provide me with opportunities to reach out to others with Your love in this place. Amen.

Go to church the first Sunday you are living in a new place. You may wish to visit several churches, but set a goal to choose one and join within six weeks to get plugged into a local body of believers as soon as possible.

■

"And the LORD, He is the One who goes before you. He will be with you, He will not leave you nor forsake you; do not fear nor be dismayed."

DEUTERONOMY 31:8 NKJV

■

Change is invigorating. If the caterpillar stayed inside the chrysalis, never daring to break out of its comfort zone, the world would have no butterflies. Don't fear change. Embrace it!

Be open to new friends in this new place that are not exactly like you or the friends you have had in the past. Certainly it is good to have some things in common with a friend, but he or she does not have to fit a certain mold.

■

If I rise on the wings of the dawn, if I settle on the far side of the sea, even there your hand will guide me, your right hand will hold me fast.

PSALM 139:9–10 NIV

■

Do something each week that will help you become more comfortable in your new environment. Put it on the calendar and follow through with it. Many people procrastinate, allowing months to pass before they establish themselves in a new place.

*Yea, though I walk through the valley of the shadow of
death, I will fear no evil: for thou art with me; thy rod
and thy staff they comfort me.*

PSALM 23:4 KJV

◼

*The LORD will protect you from all evil; He will keep
your soul. The LORD will guard your going out and your
coming in from this time forth and forever.*

PSALM 121:7–8 NASB

◼

*Take some time to just drive around and check out the
new area. Sometimes getting a little lost is the perfect
way to figure out your way around.*

After you have adjusted to your new home and feel more comfortable, do not forget how it felt to be the "new kid." Reach out to others. Welcome new students or coworkers. Take some cookies to a new neighbor.

The LORD's curse is on the house of the wicked, but he blesses the home of the righteous.

PROVERBS 3:33 NIV

Keep your thoughts and feelings about the changes you are going through and about your new environment in a journal.

■

I will lie down and sleep in peace, for you alone, O LORD, make me dwell in safety.

PSALM 4:8 NIV

■

Spruce up your new home and make it reflect your personality. Paint a room, frame some favorite photos and hang them on the walls, or hit some yard sales to find furniture you can refinish. Make the space your own. This will make it feel more like home.

*Choose for yourselves this day whom you will serve
. . .but as for me and my household, we will
serve the LORD.*

JOSHUA 24:15 NIV

■

*Go ye therefore, and teach all nations, baptizing them in
the name of the Father, and of the Son,
and of the Holy Ghost.*

MATTHEW 28:19 KJV

The Job Hunt:
Finding My Place

Unable to get any internships, I worked a lot of really terrible summer jobs throughout college. I sold fireworks, painted semitrucks, cleaned hotel rooms, walked dogs, and scrubbed swimming pools. By my junior year, I felt doomed. Who was going to hire someone like me with no professional experience whatsoever? That's when I turned to online freelance work. I found dozens of sites that offered great opportunities to graphic/web designers, writers, computer programmers, marketing gurus, and translators. And the best part was that once I had built up a reliable reputation, freelance employers started seeking me out. Not only was I gaining valuable resume experience, but I could choose what kind of work I wanted to do and how much I'd get paid for it. If only I had known about freelance opportunities sooner!

ASHLEY CASTEEL, 23

Some people grow up knowing exactly what they want to do in life. They are "born teachers," or they follow in a parent's footsteps to become a physician or a builder. Some begin working for a family business. Others are less certain of what they want to do. It can be a challenge to determine a career path, find a job, and begin working.

If you are looking for a job, take a deep breath. Remember that you are God's child, created with unique talents and abilities. The first step is to ask God to lead you. God wants to be part of your everyday life. Pray throughout the day as you are seeking employment that the Lord will open and close doors to place you in the right position.

If you are unsure of what you want to do, there are interest and career questionnaires on the Internet that may be helpful. Most universities have a career guidance department. Perhaps you have studied to prepare for a certain type of work. Regardless, you need to prepare a résumé. There are various computer programs that will take you through a step-by-step process to design a professional résumé. Include all schooling, training, and work experience (paid and volunteer) that relates to the position for which you are applying.

Search for openings online, in the newspaper, and in career placement centers. Check every day as new job postings are added regularly. Consider sending an e-mail to friends and family and let them know about your job search. You might want to attach your résumé. Networking is a great way to find a job.

If you are called for an interview, do some research in order to learn about the organization. There are several books on the market that give tips for interview preparation. It is important to be on time, or even a little bit early. It is always better to be overdressed than underdressed when making a first impression. Smile, be confident, and try to relax. Most employers will ask if you have questions at the close of the interview. Feel free to ask questions. You are learning about the company and the position just as the employer is learning about you.

When you do land a job, go out to dinner with a friend or family member and celebrate! Remember to thank God for His provision of a job for you, and if you are not already tithing, this is a great time to begin giving 10 percent of your income to kingdom work through your church.

Lord, I am new at this. Please work behind the scenes as I do my part by actively looking. I want to honor You in my work. Provide the job that You know will be the best fit for me, I pray. Amen.

*If any of you lacks wisdom, he should ask God, who
gives generously to all without finding fault,
and it will be given to him.*

JAMES 1:5 NIV

*Remember that you are informing the prospective
employer about your qualifications. It is not bragging
when you confidently state the characteristics you
possess which would make you a great employee.*

*Invest in an interview outfit appropriate for the jobs you
are applying for. This will help you to avoid the stress
of finding something to wear to an interview if you are
invited to one without much time to prepare.*

*I guide you in the way of wisdom and
lead you along straight paths.*

PROVERBS 4:11 NIV

What is man that you are mindful of him, the son of man that you care for him? You made him a little lower than the heavenly beings and crowned him with glory and honor. You made him ruler over the works of your hands; you put everything under his feet.

PSALM 8:4–6 NIV

There are different kinds of spiritual gifts, but the same Spirit is the source of them all. There are different kinds of service, but we serve the same Lord. God works in different ways, but it is the same God who does the work in all of us.

1 CORINTHIANS 12:4–6 NLT

*Pray for God to open and close doors for
you throughout your job search. Then,
trust Him when He does.*

■

*Discover what you love, chase your dream, and know
that even when you may have forgotten God, He hasn't
forgotten you. He has provided guidance, love,
and talent to you. Use those gifts to their highest ability,
and know that He is there to show you the way when
you've strayed from the path.*

NICOLE RENEE HALE, 21

■

*If it takes awhile to find a job, try to avoid
becoming discouraged. It only takes one "yes,"
but you may have to face some rejection
before you find the best fit.*

Think about the types of questions that you may be asked at an interview. You may wish to purchase an interview guidebook. Ask a friend or family member to help you practice interviewing.

■

Unless you are 100 percent sure that you want to accept a position, it is a good idea to ask for at least twenty-four hours to think it over first. Take some time to think and pray about it rather than making a rash decision.

Wait for the LORD; be strong and take heart
and wait for the LORD.

PSALM 27:14 NIV

■

Those who know your name will trust in you, for you,
LORD, have never forsaken those who seek you.

PSALM 9:10 NIV

■

Preparing a résumé is a bit tedious and time-consuming,
but it is not a task that you want to approach with
anything less than your wholehearted effort. A
professional résumé free of spelling and grammatical
errors makes a great first impression.

Trust in the LORD with all your heart and lean not on your own understanding; in all your ways acknowledge him, and he will make your paths straight.

PROVERBS 3:5–6 NIV

Do not be anxious about anything, but in everything, by prayer and petition, with thanksgiving, present your requests to God.

PHILIPPIANS 4:6 NIV

Let friends and family members know you are searching for a job. Many people find jobs through networking.

Landing the Job: Work

If you can anticipate the next step, problem, solution, or opportunity, then you will stand out and earn the respect of your boss. Look one, two, and three steps down the road instead of staring at your feet and you will be a valuable asset to the company.

TANNER COPE, 20

So, you landed a job! Sometimes after a job search ends, it takes awhile to sink in that you won't be spending your time looking for work anymore. Instead, you will be working!

Did a schoolteacher ever remind you that school was your "job"? You learned early on that you had to show up to class on time—prepared—or else things did not go well for you. It's the same with your new job. There is a time you are to show up, duties you are to perform, and a level of professionalism and courtesy you should demonstrate on the job. Ephesians 6:7 (NLT) says to work "as though you were working for the Lord rather than for people." What does this mean to you? It means that regardless of your duties, you can do them for the glory of God.

Does your attitude bring God glory? Do you stand out in the workplace as a Christian, or do you save that for Sundays?

Sometimes it can be tempting to steal from your employer. Oh, most of us are not tempted to steal monetarily, but consider these temptations. Are you tempted to leave early when the boss is not there? She'll never know. Do you send personal e-mails throughout the day and check Facebook regularly? This is robbing your employer of time for which you are being paid to work. Avoid this temptation. Work as though you are working for the Lord. Give your employer your very best.

Honesty is always the best policy. If something

you are asked to do on the job seems "fishy" to you, it most likely is. As a believer, you have the Holy Spirit as your guide. The Spirit counsels you. If you sense that nagging feeling inside that something is unethical, take heed. It may be that God is providing a way out, a chance for you to choose to do right in a situation. You may not always get ahead by doing the right thing, but you will be at peace with who you are and how you conduct yourself. This is far more important than a promotion or a bigger paycheck.

Work as unto the Lord. Respect your employer. Have a good attitude. Do your best. Be honest. Let the Spirit lead you. These are guidelines to a successful work life. Enjoy your new job!

God, thank You for my job. Help me as I seek to honor You in my work. Amen.

Change is inevitable. You will more than likely have more than one job in your adult life, multiple employers or supervisors, and a variety of roles. You may change offices, locations, or even cities. Embrace change in your work. It keeps things fresh!

■

Seek out other Christians in your workplace. Organize a morning prayer time or Bible study.

■

Yes, always use honest weights and measures, so that you may enjoy a long life in the land the LORD your God is giving you.

DEUTERONOMY 25:15 NLT

Observe the Sabbath day by keeping it holy, as the LORD your God has commanded you. Six days you shall labor and do all your work, but the seventh day is a Sabbath to the LORD your God. On it you shall not do any work.

DEUTERONOMY 5:12–14 NIV

Be on time. This honors your employer or your employees. It honors those you work with and those that you serve in your line of work.

Draw a line between your work life and your social life. Things can get complicated when your circle of friends is also your circle of colleagues.

■

He who works his land will have abundant food, but the one who chases fantasies will have his fill of poverty.

PROVERBS 28:19 NIV

■

Remember the common acronym from a few years back, WWJD? What would Jesus do? Always a good idea to keep this in mind in your work.

Organization can help you to be more effective in your job. Keep sticky notes handy. Write yourself reminders and put them in a prominent place. It is good to have a "to do" or "to deal with ASAP" bin or folder.

■

If a man is lazy, the rafters sag; if his hands are idle, the house leaks.

ECCLESIASTES 10:18 NIV

*Don't become a workaholic. Strive to reach a balance
that allows you to have a healthy lifestyle. Do not
neglect family, exercise, leisure time, hobbies,
and healthy eating. Your work is important,
but so are other aspects of your life.*

■

*Work willingly at whatever you do, as though you
were working for the Lord rather than for people.*

COLOSSIANS 3:23 NLT

■

*Commit to the LORD whatever you do,
and your plans will succeed.*

PROVERBS 16:3 NIV

Your workplace is a mission field. Jesus said that the "harvest is plentiful, but the workers are few" (Matthew 9:37 NIV). Work for the Kingdom of the Lord. Go into your office, your classroom, or your company with a heart and a boldness that points others to your Savior.

■

May the favor of the Lord our God rest upon us; establish the work of our hands for us—yes, establish the work of our hands.

PSALM 90:17 NIV

■

You will spend many hours working in your lifetime. Choose your occupation wisely. Make it something that fits your gifts and abilities well, something you see as worthy of your time and effort.

■

The LORD God took the man and put him in the Garden of Eden to work it and take care of it.

GENESIS 2:15 NIV

Getting it Done:
Time Management

It is extremely important to have balance in one's life, especially when adjusting to new circumstances and surroundings. Making time for a quiet time with Jesus every day is essential to growing in Him and seeking His will. By making sure that I put God first, He helps me to prioritize every other area in my life.

EMILY HOERNSCHEMEYER, 20

There will always be just twenty-four hours in a day. No matter how much you accomplish (or don't!), rejoice or complain, those hours will come and go. They are given to you by God to live to the fullest. Each new day of life should be celebrated as a gift.

God wants us to work. He created the world in six days, and on the seventh He rested. God did not *need* to rest. He rested so we would have an example to follow. We are to work hard, but we are also to remember when it is time to rest. Life can become unbalanced quickly if we don't hone our time-management skills.

The workweek begins with a bang. Monday morning never waits. It comes, like the finder in hide-and-seek, whether we are "ready or not!" Before you find yourself snowed under with piles of work to complete both at your job and at home, think about how you will manage your time.

Make a list. Compile all the things you need to accomplish during the coming week and organize your list in a way that works for you. Keep the list in a place where it will always be easily accessible like your purse or wallet, on your desk, or even posted on a bulletin board or on your refrigerator. As you complete the tasks, check them off your list.

Keeping a calendar is also helpful for time management. Whether it is a handheld device, a wall or desk calendar, or a daily planner, a calendar will remind you of upcoming events. As soon as you schedule a meeting, are assigned a due date, or make plans with a friend, record it on your calendar.

Besides lists and calendars, other time management helps might include thinking through your weeknights. Is it reasonable to schedule something for every weeknight? Should you consider keeping two to three nights open each week so that you can take care of laundry, housekeeping, and simply have some downtime to spend alone? Our tendency is often to schedule our lives so heavily that by the weekend, we reach a point of exhaustion. Be cautious not to do this. Proper time management will even help you to stay healthy, especially if you remember to schedule time for regular exercise and enough sleep.

Lord, teach me to manage my time in a way that will honor You. Amen.

She watches over the affairs of her household and does not eat the bread of idleness.

PROVERBS 31:27 NIV

■

If your home is getting messy throughout the week, and the weekend is nowhere in sight, try setting a kitchen timer for fifteen minutes and hold a speed-cleaning session. You will be amazed how much tidier your place will be after just a few minutes!

■

For every minute spent in organizing, an hour is earned.

UNKNOWN

Think ahead. Buy a book of stamps when you are at the post office to mail a package. While grocery shopping, double up on the items you tend to run out of quickly. This will save you some extra trips!

■

Remember that it is important to take time for your meals and for exercise. You will feel better and be more alert if you do not attempt to work around the clock. Your production at work will actually increase if you take care of yourself.

■

Don't count every hour in the day, make every hour in the day count.

UNKNOWN

Try heading for bed fifteen minutes earlier than you normally do. Resist hitting the snooze button more than one time each morning.

■

There is a time for everything, and a season for every activity under heaven.

ECCLESIASTES 3:1 NIV

■

Lost time is never found again.

BENJAMIN FRANKLIN

Set up an online bill payment program. Have insurance or other monthly payments automatically withdrawn from your bank account. Withdraw a certain amount of cash each weekend to carry you through the coming week. All of these are wise tips that will help you save time and keep you from worrying about money.

■

So then, let us not be like others, who are asleep, but let us be alert and self-controlled.

1 THESSALONIANS 5:5–7 NIV

Start each day with prayer. Ask God to help you to manage your time. When you find yourself stressed about time, ask Him to multiply your time for you. He wants to be involved in the details of your life.

■

Be a multitasker. Read while you walk on the treadmill. Make a grocery list while you wait for your car to get an oil change. Multitasking is a great time-management tool.

When you start to procrastinate, think to yourself about the outcome. You do not want to be overloaded tomorrow because you chose to do nothing today. Opt to do half of the project or task instead of not tackling it at all. This will give you a head start the next day. You may even find that once you begin, you have time to finish the job!

■

Don't say you don't have enough time. You have exactly the same number of hours per day that were given to Helen Keller, Pasteur, Michelangelo, Mother Teresa, Leonardo da Vinci, Thomas Jefferson, and Albert Einstein.

H. JACKSON BROWN JR.

Don't Give Up: Developing Perseverance

My father still keeps a suitcase filled with the (literally) hundreds of rejection letters he received when he was job hunting after he graduated college. He showed it to me my junior year when we were cleaning up the basement, and needless to say, it discouraged me. Sure, he had eventually been offered a job (the same one he's had for twenty years), but I was worried that I wouldn't be able to handle that kind of rejection. I prayed about the situation, and God helped me build up my courage and patience. And when I did finally get a job, I understood why my father had held on to all those rejection letters for so many years: to remind himself that perseverance always pays off in the end.

ASHLEY CASTEEL, 23

"Stick-to-it-iveness" is a trait possessed by many who have made a mark on the world. The ability to stand strong through trials and temporary setbacks is a must if we're going to find success in any area of life. The Bible tells us that we can do all things through Christ's strength (Philippians 4:13).

As you face hard times in your studies, your career path, or your personal life, remember that growth is often the result of trials. No one *wants* to go through trials. If only every day could be our best day! If only every attempt could end in a victory! But instead, sometimes hurdles, failures, and delays in gratification will come your way.

Have you ever spent time with an elderly Christian whom you respect? He or she undoubtedly has a life story dotted with both highs and lows. While walking through the struggles is not pleasant, God is in the business of working all things together for good. It is a promise in Romans 8:28.

James 1:2–4 (NIV) says it this way: "Consider it pure joy, my brothers, whenever you face trials of many kinds, because you know that the testing of your faith develops perseverance. Perseverance must finish its work so that you may be mature and complete, not lacking anything."

The two words *mature* and *complete* are linked together here. Completeness does not come without maturity, and maturity is the result of perseverance.

Trust the Lord to see you through tough times.

Considering trials as "pure joy" may seem like a crazy demand, but think about the reasoning behind such a statement. God sees our lives from a completely different perspective than we see them. We sit at the table looking at all the pieces, turning them over and examining them to try to imagine how they could fit together. He sees the pieces as a completed jigsaw puzzle, a beautiful picture. God knows that in order for the picture of our life to be complete, we must grow through trials.

Perseverance. Maturity. Wholeness in Christ. Be a man or woman whose life is marked by "stick-to-it-iveness." God is not finished with you yet!

I have to admit, Lord, that it is not easy to thank You for trials. But I choose to thank You. Struggles cause me to seek You in a deeper way. Be my strength where I am weak. Develop in me a strength of character that will bring You glory. Amen.

*If you get up one more time than you fall,
you will make it through.*

CHINESE PROVERB

*For this very reason, make every effort to add to your
faith goodness; and to goodness, knowledge; and to
knowledge, self-control; and to self-control, perseverance;
and to perseverance, godliness; and to godliness,
brotherly kindness; and to brotherly kindness, love.*

2 PETER 1:5–7 NIV

*Many of the great achievements of the world were
accomplished by tired and discouraged men
who kept on working.*

UNKNOWN

Watch, stand fast in the faith, be brave, be strong.
Let all that you do be done with love.

1 CORINTHIANS 16:13–14 NKJV

And we rejoice in the hope of the glory of God.
Not only so, but we also rejoice in our sufferings,
because we know that suffering produces perseverance;
perseverance, character; and character, hope.

ROMANS 5:2–4 NIV

*By faith he [Moses] left Egypt, not fearing the king's
anger; he persevered because he saw
him who is invisible.*

HEBREWS 11:27 NIV

■

*Nothing in this world can take the place of persistence.
Talent will not; nothing is more common than
unsuccessful people with talent. Genius will not;
unrewarded genius is almost a proverb. Education will
not; the world is full of educated derelicts. Persistence
and determination alone are omnipotent. The slogan
"press on" has solved and always will solve
the problems of the human race.*

CALVIN COOLIDGE

*Blessed is the man who perseveres under trial, because
when he has stood the test, he will receive the crown of
life that God has promised to those
who love him.*

JAMES 1:12 NIV

■

*We have confidence in the Lord that you are doing and
will continue to do the things we command.
May the Lord direct your hearts into
God's love and Christ's perseverance.*

2 THESSALONIANS 3:4–5 NIV

■

*Stay the course, light a star,
Change the world where'er you are.*

RICHARD LE GALLIENNE

I am not judged by the number of times I fail, but by the number of times I succeed: and the number of times I succeed is in direct proportion to the number of times I fail and keep trying.

TOM HOPKINS

■

Watch your life and doctrine closely. Persevere in them, because if you do, you will save both yourself and your hearers.

1 TIMOTHY 4:16 NIV

Brothers, as an example of patience in the face of suffering, take the prophets who spoke in the name of the Lord. As you know, we consider blessed those who have persevered. You have heard of Job's perseverance and have seen what the Lord finally brought about. The Lord is full of compassion and mercy.

JAMES 5:10–12 NIV

Stand up, stand up for Jesus,
stand in His strength alone;
The arm of flesh will fail you,
ye dare not trust your own. . .
Stand up, stand up for Jesus,
the strife will not be long;
This day the noise of battle,
the next the victor's song.

GEORGE DUFFIELD JR.
"STAND UP, STAND UP FOR JESUS"

Thicker than Water:
My Family

My family is my physical support system. They are always there to encourage me and offer me wisdom and insight. I not only trust them, but I also enjoy spending time with them and have established deep spiritual and emotional relationships with each member.

EMILY HOERNSCHEMEYER, 20

Have you ever looked at someone else's family and thought to yourself *Why can't my family be that close? That "normal"? That kind? That together?* In reality, there is no perfect family. Each has a unique blend of personalities, strengths, and weaknesses. Your family is a gift, and what you do with it is up to you.

God's Word emphasizes that we are to honor our parents. What does honoring your parents look like? It looks different now that you are a recent graduate than it did when you were a child, and yet the command remains. Honor your parents by respecting them. You may not always agree with their advice, but at least listen to it. They are God-given authorities in your life, and as you transition into adulthood, their role shifts to that of supportive friends.

To honor them also means that you should represent them well. Wherever you go and whatever you do, for as long as you live, you will represent your earthly parents. You are a reflection of them. Will your ways bring them joy or disgrace? Consider this as you make choices. Bring your family honor.

Siblings also are a gift from God. The age and personality differences between siblings affect these unique relationships. If you and your siblings are close in age or of very different dispositions, you may have experienced sibling rivalry while growing up. Now that you are older, seek to find places in those relationships that may need healing. Ask God to help you have grace with your siblings, to accept them as different from you, and to love them for who God made them to be.

Life is full of changes. Friends come and go, but your family is forever. Be cautious with how you speak to your family. You may have every reason in the world to be angry with a family member, but you can choose to love instead. Ask God to soften your heart in areas where it is hard. Sometimes it is difficult to love those closest in our lives.

Recognize that you are not part of your family by accident. God ordained these people for you to walk and grow with, belong to, and care for on this earth. He planted you in the family where you find yourself. A family is a wonderful blessing from God. A family is forever. Choose to appreciate yours. Seek to honor God in your family relationships.

Father, thank You for my family. We are a bunch of imperfect people. Help us to love one another well. Amen.

Children's children are a crown to the aged,
and parents are the pride of their children.

PROVERBS 17:6 NIV

■

Make it a part of your schedule to call home to talk to
family once a week. No matter how far away you are,
communicating with people back home on a regular
basis will keep you connected.

■

Each of you should look not only to your own interests,
but also to the interests of others.

PHILIPPIANS 2:4 NIV

*Honor your father and your mother, that your
days may be long upon the land which the
LORD your God is giving you.*

EXODUS 20:12 NKJV

■

*Large crowds were traveling with Jesus, and turning to
them he said: "If anyone comes to me and does not hate
his father and mother, his wife and children, his brothers
and sisters—yes, even his own life—he cannot be my
disciple. And anyone who does not carry his cross and
follow me cannot be my disciple.*

LUKE 14:25–27 NIV

Respect differences in personalities within your family members. People have different strengths, weaknesses, communication styles, and love languages.

■

Remember birthdays. This will mean a lot to your family. Even if you live far away, you can send a birthday card through the mail or even an e-card online.

"Which of you fathers, if your son asks for a fish, will give him a snake instead? Or if he asks for an egg, will give him a scorpion? If you then, though you are evil, know how to give good gifts to your children, how much more will your Father in heaven give the Holy Spirit to those who ask him!"

LUKE 11:11–13 NIV

■

A happy family is but an earlier heaven.

GEORGE BERNARD SHAW

I am a part of a big family and going to college was just my family expanding. I loved introducing my parents to my friends and they loved visiting and taking us out to dinner. (Free meals out are also pretty nice!) Sharing stories with your family helps them feel a part of your college experience as well as makes you feel as though you have one world instead of two.

MOLLY WEISGARBER, 22

■

In every conceivable manner, the family is link to our past, bridge to our future.

ALEX HALEY

I have never been smarter than when I've kept my mouth shut. "When words are many, sin is not absent, but he who holds his tongue is wise." Put Proverbs 10:19 into practice and you will be amazed at how many conflicts are averted and how many feelings you will not hurt.

TANNER COPE, 20

Be completely humble and gentle; be patient, bearing with one another in love.

EPHESIANS 4:2 NIV

Who I Hang With:
My Friendships

You will make friends! I promise! The first year of college all freshmen are in the same boat. I loved freshman year because it is a rare opportunity to "start over." Who you were in high school does not have to be the person you are in college. Be yourself! Try new things you normally wouldn't. College is a unique season of life where you are able to encounter so many different and unique individuals with whom you'll share the next four to five years.

MOLLY WEISGARBER, 22

How do you choose your friends? Have you come to understand that there are various types of friends, different levels of friendship, and that just a few precious friendships stand the test of time?

There are friends that you share an interest with and enjoy spending time with because of what you have in common. This may be a running buddy, a book club member, a guy on your football team, a girl you scrapbook with, or a classmate who shares your passion for photography. This type of friendship may deepen as time passes.

Other friends enter your life due to proximity, such as neighbors in your hometown or in the college dorm. Some friends you'll meet through work, church, or through other friends. Some you grew up with or have known a very long time. Have you ever been asked how you came to know a particular friend and found it hard to recall exactly how you met? It just seems that person has always been a part of your life, doesn't it?

Everyone needs friends that fill different roles. If you told your deepest, darkest secret to every friend you have, it wouldn't stay a secret long. If you have found a friend that you can trust, a friend that sticks around through the bad times as well as the good, you are blessed. Appreciate that friend. Seek to be a good friend in return. It takes being a good friend in order to have good friends.

Jesus chose friends. He walked with twelve men

known as his "disciples" during His ministry here on earth. He spoke into their lives, lived among them, ate meals with them, traveled with them, and taught them in more specific ways than He taught the masses. The calling was not an easy one for these friends of the Savior. They left houses, families, and occupations to follow Christ. They laid down their lives for His cause.

The Word of God instructs us that we are to be *in this world* but that as Christians, we are not *of this world*. Know the difference? Certainly, Jesus was a friend to the unlovely and the unlovable—and we should be, too. He taught, however, that we are to be "equally yoked" in our dealings with others. Our closest companions, business associates, and certainly those we would look to for counsel should be Christians. The worldview of an unbeliever is vastly different than that of a believer. Seek out friends who know and love Jesus, and you can be sure that they will have your best interest at heart.

God, thank You for my friends. Help me to be a good friend that I might have good friends. Amen.

Some friends are for a lifetime. Others are for a season.
Accept this fact. Hold on to the friends that are
lifelong... but appreciate those that God puts
in your life simply for a particular time.
Both are valuable treasures.

■

Do not be yoked together with unbelievers. For what do
righteousness and wickedness have in common?
Or what fellowship can light have with darkness?

2 Corinthians 6:14 niv

■

It is much easier for a friend to pull you down than
for you to pull a friend up. Make wise choices in the
company you keep. Your closest friends
should be followers of Christ.

*He who walks with wise men will be wise, but the
companion of fools will be destroyed.*

PROVERBS 13:20 NKJV

■

*I chose to attend a non-Christian university. However,
I made it a point to get invested into a small group and
establish a circle of friends who shared the same love for
the Lord that I do. Accountability is key in any stage of
life and as wonderful as college is, it's not always easy.
You need those strong sisters and brothers in
Christ to lean on.*

MOLLY WEISGARBER, 22

Dear friends, since God so loved us,
we also ought to love one another.

1 John 4:11 niv

■

A true friend will always point you to Jesus and never
lead you away from Him.

■

Let us not give up meeting together, as some are in the
habit of doing, but let us encourage one another—
and all the more as you see the Day approaching.

Hebrews 10:25 niv

*A man of many companions may come to ruin,
but there is a friend who sticks closer than a brother.*

PROVERBS 18:24 NIV

■

*Don't be afraid of silence with friends. It is good
to learn to be comfortable in another's
presence without noise.*

■

*As iron sharpens iron, so a man sharpens the
countenance of his friend.*

PROVERBS 27:17 NKJV

After graduating college, opportunities to date and meet new people often dwindle. The responsibilities of work and home can take over until there's just not enough time to actively seek the man or woman of your dreams. It may be tempting to just settle for the next best thing, but companionship for the sake of companionship is entirely too much work—especially on top of all the other stresses that go along with post-graduate life. You need trust, good communication, and someone who understands your commitments, goals, and beliefs; someone who's not out to play games. When it comes to love, God knows when you're ready for the real thing. If you wait on Him, He'll send you that perfect someone at just the right time.

ASHLEY CASTEEL, 23

■

*A friend loves at all times,
and a brother is born for adversity.*

PROVERBS 17:17 NIV

Wounds from a friend can be trusted,
but an enemy multiplies kisses.

PROVERBS 27:6 NIV

■

A true friend is the best possession.

BENJAMIN FRANKLIN

■

Choose friends that will tell you the truth
even if it is not always pleasant.

Making the Big Bucks:
Managing Money

I was wary of credit cards when I was in college. I had heard all the horror stories about variable interest rates, fees, and how long it would take to pay off. So I steered clear, but then I realized that after school, if I wanted to buy a car or get an apartment, I needed some kind of credit, so I had to break down and get one. I only used it to pay for things I knew I could pay off the following month, and that definitely helped build my credit rating.

ASHLEY CASTEEL, 23

How exciting it is to earn a paycheck! Money, however, can become a major source of stress if it is mismanaged. The loss of a good credit record will limit purchases that may be made in the future. Arguments about money are known to contribute to the breakdown of marriages. So it is important to be proactive in your approach to finances. Most adults would agree that money management is a skill they wish they had acquired sooner!

Are you a college student working to pay for coursework or to earn spending money? Maybe you're a recent graduate who is entering the workforce, and you will be covering all of your own expenses for the first time. Regardless of your situation, applying basic financial management principles is essential.

Principle number one is to tithe to your church. God promises to faithfully provide for His children when we are faithful in our tithing. He tells us in Malachi that He will "open the floodgates of heaven and pour out so much blessing that you will not have enough room for it" (Malachi 3:10 NIV). If your church provides offering envelopes, put your tithe in an envelope on the day you get your paycheck. Take it to church on the following Sunday and enjoy the blessing of giving. Giving is an act of worship, just as much so as singing or praising God. We bring Him glory and honor through giving to His kingdom work. The Bible tells us that the Lord delights in a cheerful giver.

Managing finances involves budgeting. Choose one of the many online financial programs to help you design a personal budget and keep track of your spending online. It is a good idea to record all spending for a couple of months and use this information to design a budget that includes:

- tithe
- housing
- utilities
- food
- entertainment
- clothing
- miscellaneous

Each person will have a unique budget. Typically, about one-third of your paycheck will cover your rent or mortgage payment. Utility bills will vary, depending on the type of home you live in, the time of year, and your lifestyle. Request an average bill for your apartment or house before you even move into it. What can you do to keep your electricity bill low? Such things as turning off lights and not running heat or air conditioning excessively can help with this.

Many money experts suggest saving $1,000 and placing it in a separate emergency account. When unexpected needs arise (and they always will), such as new tires for your car or dental work, your monthly budget will not be affected. When you use funds from your emergency account, replenish this "safety net" quickly. Be sure to use the money from this account only for true emergencies.

Managing finances, while it will come more naturally to some than others, can actually be rewarding and even fun!

God, as I seek to get my finances in order, give me wisdom. Help me to be a good steward of all of the resources that You have given me. Amen.

"Bring the whole tithe into the storehouse, so that there may be food in My house, and test Me now in this," says the LORD of hosts, "if I will not open for you the windows of heaven and pour out for you a blessing until it overflows."

MALACHI 3:10 NASB

Whoever loves money never has money enough; whoever loves wealth is never satisfied with his income. This too is meaningless.

ECCLESIASTES 5:10 NIV

*Avoid impulse purchases. Plan
ahead before you spend.*

■

*"Do not store up for yourselves treasures on earth, where
moth and rust destroy, and where thieves break in and
steal. But store up for yourselves treasures in heaven,
where neither moth nor rust destroys, and where thieves
do not break in or steal; for where your treasure is,
there your heart will be also."*

MATTHEW 6:19–21 NASB

■

*Look for inexpensive or even free events in your
community. There are music festivals, arts and crafts
fairs, cultural events, and outdoor concerts throughout
the year in most cities.*

Dishonest money dwindles away, but he who gathers money little by little makes it grow.

PROVERBS 13:11 NIV

■

After college, even though I had avoided credit cards, I still had a lot of debt: school loans, a car loan, wedding bills, and a mortgage. I wanted to get rid of as much of it as I could as fast as possible. It was so tempting to put my extra money toward my smaller debts—the ones I could pay off the fastest—but a good friend explained to me that a better strategy is to pay off the debt with the highest interest rate first. I did the math and realized this was right—in the long run, I'd ultimately be saving more money by following that advice.

ASHLEY CASTEEL, 23

*Little things can make a big difference in your budget.
For example, purchasing twelve-packs of soft drinks
rather than buying that soda for $1 each day from a
machine can save you up to $7 per week, which is $28
per month and $336 per year.*

■

*"No servant can serve two masters. Either he will hate
the one and love the other, or he will be devoted
to the one and despise the other. You cannot
serve both God and Money."*

LUKE 16:13 NIV

*Let no debt remain outstanding, except the continuing
debt to love one another, for he who
loves his fellowman has fulfilled the law.*

ROMANS 13:8 NIV

■

*If you have a credit card that has a high interest rate,
make a phone call to the company and request a lower
one. Normally you can get at least a small decrease in
interest simply through taking the time to ask.*

If you are a college or graduate student, ask your bank about a student checking account. Banks often waive certain fees and offer special benefits for students.

■

Once I was young, and now I am old. Yet I have never seen the godly abandoned or their children begging for bread. The godly always give generous loans to others, and their children are a blessing.

PSALM 37:25–26 NLT

■

Cooking at home with friends can be a lot of fun. It also saves money. Eating out really adds up if you do it too often.

Talking with My Heavenly Father: Prayer

Alone time is hard to come across once classes get started and you become invested in new activities/clubs, and your friends. To "escape," all I need is my iPod and my journal. I love to write down my prayers as letters to God because it keeps me focused and is a great way to look back and see how God is working through different seasons of my life.

MOLLY WEISGARBER, 22

How many text messages and e-mails do you send in an average week? More than a hundred? Technology allows us to communicate constantly with our friends and family members. Cell phones and computers are wonderful tools for staying connected even with far-away loved ones.

Think about your communication with God. Is it as frequent? The Bible tells us to "pray continually." Do you spend time with God? Do you talk with Him, listen to Him, and seek Him in all things? It's easy to get so busy that prayer loses its priority in your life. God is pleased when you put relating to Him high on your list.

Have you set a particular time and place to meet with God on a regular basis? If you find it hard to focus during prayer times, you might try the ACTS acronym.

Express *adoration*. Praise God. This is different from *thanking* God in that adoration is telling God how much He means to you, not for what He has done but simply for *who He is*. Try praising the Lord by speaking scripture back to Him:

"God, You are the same yesterday, today, and tomorrow. Holy, holy, holy is the Lord God Almighty. You are above all things. You are perfect in every way."

Praise Him by speaking His names:

"Heavenly Father, Creator, God, Jehovah, my Jesus, Emmanuel—God with us, the Great I Am, Savior, Yahweh."

Next, **confess** your sins to God. God already knows your sins, but it is good to come before Him and willingly confess your sins. Agree with God that sin hinders your fellowship with Him and with others. He is a *loving Father* who is so willing to forgive you when you ask. At the same time, He is a *holy God*. He calls believers to confess their sins and to turn from them, daily seeking to be more like Jesus.

After confession, express **thanksgiving** to God. Thank Him for the blessings He has poured out on you. Thank Him for His provisions, His gifts, and for your salvation through Jesus' blood which was shed for you on the cross.

Finally, **supplication** is presenting your requests to God. You can pray for your own needs and for the needs of others. There will be times when you may not even know what to pray. The Bible assures us that the Holy Spirit prays for us at such times. Simply speak the name of Jesus. Present your requests to the Lord. Cast your cares upon Him.

Remember to be still before the Lord. If you do all the talking, God does not have a chance to work in your spirit. Some of the greatest direction and comfort come to God's children when they take time to rest in Him and listen for His still small voice.

Father, hear my prayers, I ask,
and teach me to listen to you. Amen

*The LORD is far from the wicked, but he
hears the prayer of the righteous.*

PROVERBS 15:29 NIV

■

*God does not need your prayers to be filled
with ornate language. He is interested
in a humble heart and a sweet spirit.*

■

*In the morning, O LORD, you hear my voice;
in the morning I lay my requests before
you and wait in expectation.*

PSALM 5:3 NIV

*When you tell a friend that you will pray for him or her,
follow through with your promise. In fact, ask if you can
pray for the need right then and there. Just
stop wherever you are and pray over your friend.
There is great power in agreeing in prayer.*

■

*For where two or three are gathered together in my
name, there am I in the midst of them.*

MATTHEW 18:20 KJV

■

*Make a photo flip-book of pictures of family members,
friends, and missionaries. Use the photos during prayer
times. You may divide the book into sections and pray
for certain individuals on different days of the week.
The flip-book can be arranged in a way
that works best for you.*

Now when Daniel learned that the decree had been published, he went home to his upstairs room where the windows opened toward Jerusalem. Three times a day he got down on his knees and prayed, giving thanks to his God, just as he had done before.

DANIEL 6:10 NIV

To be a Christian without prayer is no more possible than to be alive without breathing.

MARTIN LUTHER KING JR.

The LORD detests the sacrifice of the wicked,
but the prayer of the upright pleases him.

PROVERBS 15:8 NIV

■

There is not a set time, date, or place to talk to
God. Talk to Him constantly and as
personally as your best friend.

EMILY HOERNSCHEMEYER, 20

■

Grant that I may not pray alone with the mouth;
help me that I may pray from the depths of my heart.

MARTIN LUTHER

Be joyful always; pray continually; give thanks in all circumstances, for this is God's will for you in Christ Jesus.

1 THESSALONIANS 5:16–18 NIV

◼

Pray as though everything depended on God. Work as though everything depended on you.

SAINT AUGUSTINE

◼

The effectual fervent prayer of a righteous man availeth much.

JAMES 5:16 KJV

And when you pray, do not keep on babbling like pagans, for they think they will be heard because of their many words. Do not be like them, for your Father knows what you need before you ask him.

MATTHEW 6:7–8 NIV

Make Me a Servant: Serving Others

When I was in school, it was so easy to find service projects to get involved in. The bloodmobile came to campus and some of my classes were organized around service projects. There were always weekend trips the school offered to nursing homes, churches, and schools. I never had to go out of my way to serve others. It wasn't until I graduated that I realized how much I had taken that for granted. Now I have to work around my work schedule, finances, and find my own ways to serve—but in many ways that makes the service work I'm doing now much more personally fulfilling.

ASHLEY CASTEEL, 23

The word *service* shows up in church a lot. The pastor asks for us to serve in the nursery. The bulletin advertises a need for people to serve as parking attendants and children's choir directors. Missionaries serve in Africa, China, and even right here at home in our own country. *Serving* is used in other contexts also. We serve food to guests and tennis balls to opponents. So what does *service* mean, and what does it have to do with you?

Christ Jesus taught that the least would be greatest. He modeled putting others ahead of Himself. He washed feet, turned water to wine, and helped, healed, and blessed those He came into contact with everywhere. He was a King, and yet He didn't come to earth demanding a palace and a throne. Our Savior came to us as Emmanuel, meaning "God with us." He came humbly, served humbly, and loved people with a greater love than this world had ever known.

So, how can you follow Jesus' example? How can you be a servant? After all, your schedule is packed. You may have classes as well as a full- or part-time job. You are juggling a professional and a personal life. You are new at the office and expected to put in a lot of extra hours.

Serving can be simple. Start small and choose an area that interests you where you can start serving. God has made you unique in your personality, strengths, and passions. If you love animals, use this to help others. There are ministries in many communities and churches that take dogs and puppies into nursing homes or hospitals to cheer the patients. Do you enjoy working with children? There is always a need for childcare so that parents can attend services and Bible classes in church or at apartment ministries. Serving can mean visiting a homebound friend or filling soup bowls at a homeless shelter. It will grow as you discover the blessings of being a servant for the Kingdom of Jesus. You may one day start a new ministry in your church or establish a Bible study at your company! But even the smallest acts of service never go unnoticed by God, and you will be richly blessed through the act of giving to others.

God, thank You for opportunities to serve You by serving others. Give me a servant's heart, I pray. Amen.

"So when you give to the needy, do not announce it with trumpets, as the hypocrites do in the synagogues and on the streets, to be honored by men. I tell you the truth, they have received their reward in full. But when you give to the needy, do not let your left hand know what your right hand is doing, so that your giving may be in secret. Then your Father, who sees what is done in secret, will reward you."

MATTHEW 6:2–4 NIV

Make a habit of thanking those that serve you.
Waiters and waitresses, store clerks, teachers,
families, and custodians need to know
that you appreciate their service.

Service involves time. To serve requires that you trade in some "you time" and make it "others time." Do you have a free hour or two per week? Serve the Lord. It will become the time of your week that you look forward to the most!

■

"A new command I give you: Love one another. As I have loved you, so you must love one another. By this all men will know that you are my disciples, if you love one another."

JOHN 13:34–35 NIV

The entire law is summed up in a single command:
"Love your neighbor as yourself."

GALATIANS 5:14 NIV

■

I expect to pass through this world but once; any good
thing therefore that I can do, or any kindness that I can
show to any fellow creature, let me do it now;
let me not defer or neglect it, for I shall
not pass this way again.

STEPHAN GRELLET

■

Pure and undefiled religion in the sight of our God and
Father is this: to visit orphans and widows in their
distress, and to keep oneself unstained by the world.

JAMES 1:27 NASB

*Serve for the sake of love, for the sake of service—
not for a pat on the back or a thank-you. Service
done in secret is especially pleasing to the Lord.*

■

*If anyone serves, he should do it with the strength
God provides, so that in all things God may be praised
through Jesus Christ. To him be the glory and the power
for ever and ever. Amen.*

1 PETER 4:11 NIV

Serve those that you work with on a daily basis. Fill a coffee cup. Cover a class. Pick up a shift. Share a word of encouragement. In doing so, you may be the only Jesus that co-worker ever sees.

■

You, my brothers, were called to be free. But do not use your freedom to indulge the sinful nature; rather, serve one another in love. The entire law is summed up in a single command: "Love your neighbor as yourself."

Galatians 5:13–14 niv

Jesus called them together and said, ". . .Whoever wants to become great among you must be your servant, and whoever wants to be first must be your slave—just as the Son of Man did not come to be served, but to serve, and to give his life as a ransom for many."

MATTHEW 20:25–28 NIV

■

Each one should use whatever gift he has received to serve others, faithfully administering God's grace in its various forms.

1 PETER 4:10 NIV

Playing Nice: The Importance of Forgiveness

I've been reminded many times throughout my college years of God's command to forgive, no matter how badly the grievance has hurt you. It can be extremely difficult, but in the end, the relationship is always stronger, and the forgiveness is always worth it—especially if the other person is your roommate or hall mate.

AMANDA WEIDMAN, 21

Grace. It is a word we sing about. It is in many well-known songs and hymns. It is a word that is present in many scriptures that even young children memorize in Sunday School classes. Do we really grasp its meaning, though? What is grace?

Grace has been defined as "unmerited favor." It is not earned. It is a gift. God demonstrated amazing grace when He sacrificed His only son Jesus for us on the cross. Through Jesus, we are forgiven of our sins. Ephesians 2:8–9 (NIV) says, "It is by grace you have been saved. . .not by works that any man should boast." We do not do anything to achieve salvation other than to believe and accept God's grace.

We have been shown grace. And it's because we have been shown this grace that we must also show it to others. It is not always easy to forgive. Intentionally or unintentionally, others will hurt us—it's a fact. Some level of hurt, rejection, and disappointment is inevitable if we are to exist in relationship with others. So it is so important that we learn to forgive.

Forgiveness does not mean that you accept what was done to you and agree that it was okay. In fact, it is quite the opposite. It means that although you *know* what was done to you was not right, you *choose* to pardon the offender. You choose to be merciful.

The Bible is very clear about forgiveness. Jesus said that we should forgive our neighbors seventy times seven, implying that our forgiveness should be unlimited. As Christians, we should be known as those who are quick to forgive, setting an example for others.

In your work, with your family and friends, and as you live in and among others in your community, you will encounter times when you can forgive or you can get angry, gossip, and claim your rights as the victim. One option will tie you down in bitterness, while the other will free you to live life unencumbered. Choose forgiveness. It is always the best choice.

Father, I have been forgiven much.
Help me, in turn, to forgive. Amen.

There is no love without forgiveness,
and there is no forgiveness without love.

BRYANT H. MCGILL

■

Satan despises forgiveness. There's nothing he
likes more than to see God's children involved in
disagreements. Satan is all about barriers and
selfishness. Jesus is all about selflessness and forgiveness.
Who will you honor with your choices when it comes
to forgiving others—the prince of this
world or the Prince of Peace?

Then Peter came and said to Him, "Lord, how often shall my brother sin against me and I forgive him? Up to seven times?" Jesus said to him, "I do not say to you, up to seven times, but up to seventy times seven."

MATTHEW 18:21–22 NASB

■

To forgive is the highest, most beautiful form of love. In return, you will receive untold peace and happiness.

ROBERT MULLER

*When we were overwhelmed by sins,
you forgave our transgressions.*

PSALM 65:3 NIV

■

Forgiveness is the oil of relationships.

JOSH MCDOWELL

■

*Forgive us our sins, as we have forgiven
those who sin against us.*

MATTHEW 6:12 NLT

Sensible people control their temper; they earn respect by overlooking wrongs.

PROVERBS 19:11 NLT

■

When you find it hard to forgive, pray that God will give you a heart of forgiveness.

■

Above all, love each other deeply, because love covers over a multitude of sins.

1 PETER 4:8 NIV

Forgiveness does not change the past,
but it does enlarge the future.

PAUL BOESE

■

Do not condemn, and you will not be condemned.
Forgive, and you will be forgiven. Give, and it will be
given to you. A good measure, pressed down, shaken
together and running over, will be poured into your lap.
For with the measure you use, it will be measured to you.

LUKE 6:36–38 NIV

*As far as the east is from the west, so far has he
removed our transgressions from us.*

PSALM 103:12 NIV

■

*Therefore I tell you, whatever you ask for in prayer,
believe that you have received it, and it will be yours.
And when you stand praying, if you hold anything
against anyone, forgive him, so that your Father in
heaven may forgive you your sins.*

MARK 11:24–25 NIV

Take a Deep Breath:
Finding Peace

I have found that sometimes simply praying for peace is the only thing that can get me through a situation. When things are going bad, I do not know what to ask for, and I don't have any clue what God is trying to teach or reveal to me. But, praying for peace calms me down and allows me to think clearly. The anger settles down, the sadness goes away, and God's still, small voice is able to get through.

ELLEN WORSHAM, 19

Peace is one of the most sought-after commodities in today's world. Some people try to find it in relationships, while others bury their troubles in alcohol or drugs. None of these things can truly deliver peace, but those who don't know Jesus can't see this. Sometimes even believers lose sight of the source of peace, but we must return to it if we are to live the abundant life God desires for us.

God grants a peace unlike any peace the world can offer. He freely gives a peace that passes all understanding, a deep abiding peace even in times of trouble. Have you ever witnessed a family that is dealing with a difficult trial, and yet faces it with amazing strength? That kind of strength is supernatural. It comes through faith in Christ. God's peace works the same way. There are no test results that can steal this type of peace. There is no bad news, rejection, or failure capable of robbing a heart that has the peace of Jesus.

For centuries, God's people have rested in peace at night despite circumstances that appeared unbearable. King David hid in caves and ran for his life, yet he found peace in the Lord. Noah was ridiculed for building an ark, but he just kept hammering. Armies have marched into battle under the banner of God's peace even when they fought against the strongest of enemies. We are no different today. We can choose peace in the face of pain and even uncertainty. God offers it. We must simply accept it—a free gift, just like His grace.

How do you find this peace? Breathe deep. Be still. Know that He is God. Your sovereign maker holds the entire universe in His hands. Surely He can manage the details of your dilemma and calm the confusion of your situation.

Peace is hard to find with music blaring, text messages ringing, and e-mails going out. Experiencing God while you are playing video games is tough. Seek solitude. Ask God to meet with you on the porch, in your prayer closet, or as you kneel beside your bed. Ask Him for rest, comfort, and for healing of the wounded parts of your spirit. Tell God you want Him to replace your rebellion with submission, your will with His, and your anxiety with His peace. Ask Him to hug you, to hold you. You will experience His peace as you read the Psalms, as you sing praise to Him, and as you quiet your soul before Him. Peace is a treasure. Value it as such, and you will never be without it again.

Jesus, my Prince of Peace, be my rest.
Be my peace. I need You so. Amen.

*Oh, love the L*ORD*, all you His saints! For the L*ORD
*preserves the faithful, and fully repays the proud
person. Be of good courage, and He shall strengthen
your heart, all you who hope in the L*ORD*.*

PSALM 31:23–24 NKJV

*"Come to me, all you who are weary and burdened, and
I will give you rest. Take my yoke upon you and learn
from me, for I am gentle and humble in heart, and you
will find rest for your souls. For my yoke
is easy and my burden is light."*

MATTHEW 11:28–30 NIV

*Peace cannot be purchased. It is free. It cannot be
earned. It is yours for the taking. Ask your Abba
Father, your Daddy, your loving God. . .and He will
plant in your heart a peace that cannot be reckoned
with. It is a gift. Stop searching. Accept it.*

*Do not be anxious about anything, but in everything,
by prayer and petition, with thanksgiving, present
your requests to God. And the peace of God, which
transcends all understanding, will guard your hearts and
your minds in Christ Jesus.*

PHILIPPIANS 4:6–7 NIV

Peace is not found in the world. It is a rare and precious gift that is apparent in the believer's life. True peace cannot be experienced without Jesus in your heart.

■

When peace, like a river, attendeth my way,
When sorrows like sea billows roll;
Whatever my lot, Thou hast taught me to say,
"It is well, it is well with my soul."

HORATIO G. SPAFFORD,
"IT IS WELL WITH MY SOUL"

Can it be that peace is not understood, not fully, by one who has never experienced unrest? To even once know confusion reveals to a soul the opposite—the sweet, calming peace of Jesus. To have been void of peace causes us to savor its sweetness all the more.

I will lie down and sleep in peace, for you alone, O LORD, make me dwell in safety.

PSALM 4:8 NIV

You can't rush through your entire day and expect to sense God's peace. You must set aside time to rest in Him, talk with Him, and listen to Him. Only then will you find His peace that passes all understanding.

"The LORD bless you and keep you; the LORD make his face shine upon you and be gracious to you; the LORD turn his face toward you and give you peace."

NUMBERS 6:24–26 NIV

■

Grace to you and peace from God our Father and the Lord Jesus Christ.

PHILEMON 1:3 NIV

■

Pray for peace. World peace. National peace. Peace within your community, your workplace, your school. Pray for peace in your family and in your heart. God is the giver of all peace. Pray for it. Pray earnestly. He will hear you, and He will provide the peace you seek.

*Peacemakers who sow in peace raise a
harvest of righteousness.*

JAMES 3:18 NIV

■

*College is wonderful but is also very stressful and it is
critical for me to retreat from the world to rejuvenate
my spirit. There is a prayer room where I go to be
alone, journal, paint, or write prayers on the wall at my
university. Or sometimes for me it means grabbing one
of my good friends, walking away from the books and
doing a late-night ice cream run, coffee shop date,
or dinner out. Those breaks off campus
are critical to relieve stress!*

MOLLY WEISGARBER, 22

He Deserves My Praise: Worship

One of the girls I go to school with does not have a great voice, but every time she opens her mouth to sing, she pours out her heart to God in worship. It made me realize that it does not matter what I look like or sound like when I am worshipping. As long as I am doing it with all my heart, God will see it as a joyful noise unto Him. I should not be worried about what others think of me and my worship style.

ELLEN WORSHAM, 19

The Bible says if we do not worship the Lord, the rocks will cry out. Can you imagine rocks having to do the work of God's people?

So what do we do? We worship the one true God, who deserves our praise. And what does worship look like? It can be as quiet as a head bowed in silent prayer and as magnificent as a thousand-person choir lifting up its voice. Worship has very few limits besides its focus. The *focus* of our worship should always be the King.

Make your life an act of worship. Speak the name of Jesus daily. Shine His light into a dark world. Sing your heart out. Dance before Him. Play an instrument. Whisper thanksgiving. Even rest can be an act of worship. God longs for you to rest in His presence rather than rush through life and miss Him.

How do you worship? Examine your personality, style, talents, and personal relationship with Jesus. These will come together in a manner that fits who you are and proclaims who He is.

Praise the Lord, all His people! Praise Him in a million different ways. Praise Him with the powerful words of traditional hymns in your Sunday best. Praise Him in blue jeans at church on Saturday night. Worship Him with offerings of tithes, time, or talents. Be creative in your praise. And before you judge another's worship style, consider God's perspective. If someone worships Him with banners or tambourines, is that okay? If another chooses to light a candle or kneel down before Him, would you stop them? Will God receive their gift of worship? Certainly! Our God is not a stuffy ruler who has strict guidelines regarding worship. He takes great joy in any form of worship you give.

It is not nearly as important *how* you worship as it is that you simply *worship*. One day we will stand before Him in heaven, and we will worship Him together with every instrument and song, every prayer, dance, and hymn! We will bow and dance and pray and sing and shout before King Jesus! Get started now. Live an abundant life of worship on this earth. This is just prep school for heaven!

Oh, Father, I long for the day we will sing and praise Your name together in heaven. Until then, let us accept that there are various ways to worship. Unify us as we praise You, each in our own way. Amen.

Praise Him on good days, and praise Him when you cannot even find the words because your heart is so broken. Praising your heavenly Father does your heart and soul so much good.

■

Praise the LORD. Praise God in his sanctuary; praise him in his mighty heavens. Praise him for his acts of power; praise him for his surpassing greatness.

PSALM 150:1–2 NIV

■

Christians come from all sorts of cultural backgrounds and differ in worship style preferences. Make a conscious decision not to judge those who worship differently from you. There is not just one "right way" to praise our God.

Let everything that has breath
praise the LORD. Praise the LORD.

PSALM 150:6 NIV

■

At school I discovered that I can worship my Lord in
many other ways than just singing at church. Drawing,
painting in my journals, coffee dates encouraging sisters
in Christ, and using the gift of dance are just some of
the many ways He has given me to worship Him.

MOLLY WEISGARBER, 22

■

Therefore I urge you, brethren, by the mercies of God, to
present your bodies a living and holy sacrifice, acceptable
to God, which is your spiritual service of worship.

ROMANS 12:1 NASB

Some of the very best worship happens when you become still before God and simply rest in the peace that only comes through Him. Express your heart to Him. Tell Him how much He means to you.

■

The trumpeters and singers joined in unison, as with one voice, to give praise and thanks to the LORD. Accompanied by trumpets, cymbals and other instruments, they raised their voices in praise to the LORD and sang: "He is good; his love endures forever." Then the temple of the LORD was filled with a cloud.

2 CHRONICLES 5:13 NIV

Listen to praise and worship music. Wake up to it. Go to sleep to it. Sing along. Close your eyes. Listen. Dwell upon the offering of praise through melodies and words. Weep. Feel. Rest. God loves it when you worship Him.

■

You must worship no other gods, for the LORD, whose very name is Jealous, is a God who is jealous about his relationship with you

EXODUS 34:14 NLT

■

*Praise him with the sounding of the trumpet,
praise him with the harp and lyre,
Praise him with tambourine and dancing,
praise him with the strings and flute,
Praise him with the clash of cymbals,
praise him with resounding cymbals.*

PSALM 150:3–5 NIV

Ask God to give you a hunger and thirst for worship
that you might become a believer who is always
entering into His presence to give Him praise,
regardless of your circumstances.

Jesus said to him, "Away from me, Satan!
For it is written: 'Worship the Lord
your God, and serve him only.'"

MATTHEW 4:10 NIV

The simplest act can be an act of worship. A gift given in the name of Jesus is worship. A smile, a kind word spoken, a head bowed before a meal, and even silence are forms of worship.

Oh come, let us worship and bow down;
Let us kneel before the LORD our Maker.

PSALM 95:6 NKJV

Do not wait until Sunday when you "go to worship." Worship every day. Worship in your car on the way to work. Worship in quiet meditation and through song and dance. Worship does not require a praise band or a pipe organ. It can happen anywhere, anytime. Praise the Lord.

Into the Unknown:
My Future

A verse that has always brought peace and confidence when I begin to worry about future decisions is Philippians 1:6 NIV: "[Be] confident of this, that he who began a good work in you will carry it on to completion until the day of Christ Jesus."

MOLLY WEISGARBER, 22

Setting out on a long road trip without a map or a GPS would be a bit unsettling, particularly to people who do not like to stop and ask for directions. But the truth is, life on earth is a journey with little direction! There was no map sent home with you from the hospital at birth that plotted out the roads you should travel through your school years and into adulthood. A lot of it may seem like guesswork, but not for the Christian. God has given us a guidebook called the Bible. He has offered us a guide to direct us in His wise and loving Holy Spirit. His commands provide an outline. Through prayer and fellowship with Him, the Lord fills in the gaps so that we might know where to go and what to do along the way.

Even so, facing an uncertain future can be frightening. We have to submit our weakness and our fear to God, trusting Him to take care of us one day at a time. He will never reveal to us more than we need to know in the moment. His children have to trust in the dark what He has proven to them in the light. He is faithful; He cannot be anything less. Base your trust in Him for your future on what God has shown you in the past.

In Bible times, God's chosen people would build an altar at the spot where God showed Himself faithful. The altar served as a reminder for them and for their children that the Lord of the universe had provided and would continue to provide for them. Build some altars in your own life. When God proves

Himself faithful to you, write it down. Mark the date and the answer to prayer or the miracle that He gave to you. As you face uncertain times and step into a future that you cannot predict, you will do so with greater peace if you can reflect on the milestones of God's faithfulness.

The Bible points out that if human parents know how to give good gifts to their children, then, of course, our heavenly Father knows what we need and how to bless us! God is out for your best interest. Nothing will happen to you in the present or in the future that has not first been filtered through His fingers. Rest in that, and face the future with joy in your heart.

Heavenly Father, direc each step that I take as I walk into the future. Help me to trust you with tomorrow.

For I am convinced that neither death nor life, neither angels nor demons, neither the present nor the future, nor any powers, neither height nor depth, nor anything else in all creation, will be able to separate us from the love of God that is in Christ Jesus our Lord.

ROMANS 8:38–39 NIV

Give all your worries and cares to God, for he cares about you.

1 PETER 5:7 NLT

"For I know the plans I have for you," declares the LORD, "plans to prosper you and not to harm you, plans to give you hope and a future."

JEREMIAH 29:11 NIV

"So don't worry about these things, saying, 'What will we eat? What will we drink? What will we wear?' These things dominate the thoughts of unbelievers, but your heavenly Father already knows all your needs. Seek the Kingdom of God above all else, and live righteously, and he will give you everything you need."

MATTHEW 6:31–33 NLT

The days of the blameless are known to the LORD, and their inheritance will endure forever. In times of disaster they will not wither; in days of famine they will enjoy plenty. But the wicked will perish.

PSALM 37:18–20 NIV

I know, O LORD, that a man's life is not his own;
it is not for man to direct his steps.

JEREMIAH 10:23 NIV

I underestimated the value of long-term goals when
I was in college. I knew they were important, but the
actual reality of their importance was diminished by
my instructors' and advisors' assurances that I could do
whatever I wanted, take my time figuring it out, and that
I didn't have to decide right away. But when you follow
that kind of advice, it leads to so much anxiety and
uncertainty. I think a better way to go about planning
for the future is to have several long-term goals or life
scenarios in mind that you'd like to achieve. Committing
yourself to a clear direction and knowing what's really
going to make you happy makes a huge difference.

ASHLEY CASTEEL, 23

Stop acting as if life is a rehearsal. Live this day as if it were your last. The past is over and gone. The future is not guaranteed.

WAYNE DYER

■

If fear of the future had overtaken them, Ruth would have left Naomi alone, Noah would never have built the ark, and Daniel certainly would have bowed to King Nebuchadnezzar. Trust the Lord in the same way that believers who came before you trusted Him with the future.

■

Each new day, submit your steps to Jesus. Ask that He reveal to you what you need to know for that day and give you the strength to honor Him in all things. If you take it one day at a time, the future will seem much less daunting.

All the days ordained for me were written in your book before one of them came to be.

PSALM 139:16 NIV

■

The same God who has held the world together in the past holds it in the palm of His hand today.
Until He determines otherwise, the sun will rise and set each new day. When Jesus returns, He will gather His own unto Himself and take us up into heaven with Him. Wow, what a future we have to look forward to!

■

Therefore do not worry about tomorrow, for tomorrow will worry about itself. Each day has enough trouble of its own.

MATTHEW 6:34 NIV

Have you considered that it actually insults God when you worry about your future? He has promised you that He will take care of it. Would you want someone to question you again and again about a promise you had made? Instead, would you not want that person to trust you?

■

The LORD will fulfill his purpose for me; your love, O LORD, endures forever—do not abandon the works of your hands.

PSALM 138:8 NIV

■

You can't change the past, but you can ruin the present by worrying about the future.

UNKNOWN

SCRIPTURE INDEX